THE CUBAN MISSILE CRISIS

Charlie Samuels

Gareth Stevens
Publishing

Please visit our website, www.garethstevens.com. For a free color catalog of all our high-quality books, call toll-free 1-800-542-2595 or fax 1-877-542-2596.

Library of Congress Cataloging-in-Publication Data

Samuels, Charlie.
The Cuban Missile Crisis / by Charlie Samuels.
  p. cm. — (Turning points in US military history)
Includes index.
ISBN 978-1-4824-0430-2 (pbk.)
ISBN 978-1-4824-3314-2 (6-pack)
ISBN 978-1-4824-0431-9 (library binding)
1. Cuban Missile Crisis, 1962 — Juvenile literature. 2. Cuba — History — 1959-1990 — Juvenile literature. 3. Cuba — Relations — United States — Juvenile literature. I. Samuels, Charlie, 1961-. II. Title.
E841.S26 2014
973.922—dc23

Published in 2014 by
Gareth Stevens Publishing
111 East 14th Street, Suite 349
New York, NY 10003

© 2014 Brown Bear Books Ltd

For Brown Bear Books Ltd:
Editorial Director: Lindsey Lowe
Managing Editor: Tim Cooke
Children's Publisher: Anne O'Daly
Design Manager: Keith Davis
Designer: Lynne Lennon
Picture Manager: Sophie Mortimer
Production Director: Alastair Gourlay

Picture Credits:
Front Cover: Getty Images: Hulton Archive

Interior: All images Robert Hunt Library except: Getty Images: Hulton Archive 11; **JFK Library:** 25, 26, 30, 31, 32, 33; **Library of Congress:** 5tr, 28, 35, 37; **Topfoto:** 38, 39; **US Department of Defense:** 19, 34, 41.

All Artworks © Brown Bear Books Ltd

Brown Bear Books has made every attempt to contact the copyright holder. If you have any information please contact smortimer@brownbearbooks.co.uk

Manufactured in the United States of America

CPSIA compliance information: Batch #CW14GS. For further information contact Gareth Stevens, New York, New York at 1-800-542-2595.

CONTENTS

INTRODUCTION

To many Americans and international observers, the crisis that faced the United States in fall 1962 threatened the world with something almost unthinkable: a nuclear war that could potentially destroy civilization.

The Cold War World

Since World War II had ended in 1945, the United States and the communist Soviet Union had competed to gain influence around the world. This period was known as the Cold War. Most of the time, the conflict was an ideological war of words. At other times, however, forces allied to the "Free World" clashed with forces backed by the communist Soviets and their Chinese allies. Meanwhile, both sides stockpiled larger and larger long-range nuclear missiles.

A Diplomatic Challenge

In October 1962, US spy planes spotted Soviet nuclear missiles (ICBMs) being set up at sites in Cuba, only 90 miles (145 km) from Florida. From there, the Soviets could easily strike the United States. President John F. Kennedy and his advisors had to make a decision. They could not allow the weapons to remain in Cuba—but aggression toward the Soviets ran the risk of starting a nuclear conflict that would wipe out millions of people. For the first time, a war in which both sides had nuclear arms seemed not just possible but highly likely.

Soviet leader Nikita Khrushchev visits the United Nations in September 1960. He began the crisis by sending missiles to Cuba.

An atomic bomb creates a mushroom cloud. The Cuban Missile Crisis took place in the shadow of a possible nuclear war.

The Cold War

With the ending of World War II in 1945, the Western Allies and the Soviet Union divided Europe between themselves. The two sides grew increasingly suspicious of each other, as the Soviets imposed Communist government on Eastern Europe. The standoff between the different blocs was known as the Cold War.

During World War II, the two different sides had come together as allies to defeat Nazi Germany. But the differences between them remained. The Soviet Union was a totalitarian state run by the Communist Party. The Soviet system was based on socialism and a

The Berlin Wall was built in August 1961 to divide the German capital in two. The wall became a powerful symbol of the Cold War.

A giant nuclear missile is driven through Red Square in Moscow in 1964 as part of the annual parade of Soviet military strength.

command economy, in which the government told everyone what to do. The United States stood for the free market and liberal democracy. Both believed that their own system was right and the other was wrong. At the end of World War II, these two superpowers dominated the world. The stage was set for a confrontation.

Hot or Cold?

For the next decades, both sides attempted to spread their influence around the world at the expense of the other. The struggle was called a

THE RED SCARE

American fears that the communists wanted to take over the world were not as unfounded as they might seem. The Soviet leader Joseph Stalin had installed communist rulers in East Germany, Poland, Hungary, Czechoslovakia, and the Baltic states. In China Mao Zedong had created a communist state. In Asia both North Korea and North Vietnam had become communist. Some African leaders were also drawn to communist ideologies. America's own backyard, Latin America, might be next.

"cold war" rather than a "hot war" because there was almost no direct armed conflict between the two superpowers. Instead, they both built up alliances; when their allies went to war, they were quick to supply arms to the opposing sides.

Fear of Communism

Many Americans had a great fear of communism. They believed that the Soviet Union was committed to spreading communism throughout the world and worried that it was a threat to US freedoms and ways of life. On the other side, the Soviets argued that their control of Eastern Europe and other states was motivated largely by the need to defend themselves against another invasion by the Western powers, like that launched by the Germans during World War II in 1942.

The two leading figures of the Cuban Missile Crisis, President John F. Kennedy and Nikita Khrushchev, met only once, in June 1961.

Soviet ballistic missiles could strike at the United States, but would take time to reach their targets from within the Soviet Union.

Nuclear Armament

What made the Cold War potentially dangerous was that both sides had long-range missiles capable of carrying nuclear weapons. There was an uneasy balance. Both nations could devastate the other, but both understood that if they fired their own missiles, the other side would fire theirs. Both countries would be destroyed.

This balance led to growing nuclear arsenals on both sides. It also meant that a direct conflict between the two superpowers might be disastrous.

NUCLEAR ARMS RACE

Although the nuclear bomb was invented in the United States, by the late 1950s the Soviets seemed to be winning the nuclear race. They were also winning the space race: they launched the Sputnik satellite in 1957 and Yuri Gagarin became the first human to orbit Earth in April 1961. Soviet leader Nikita Khrushchev boasted the Russians were producing ICBMs "like sausages." The United States rapidly escalated its own arms program.

Revolution in Cuba

ENTRADA A LA HABANA 8 DE ENERO DE 1959

This detail from a Cuban banknote celebrates the arrival of the rebels in the capital, Havana, to take control of the government.

The island of Cuba lies just 90 miles (145 km) south of Florida. Its location meant that Cuba's history was closely entwined with that of North America. This all changed in 1959, when Fidel Castro led a revolution against the dictator Fulgencio Batista.

In 1898, the United States defeated Spain in the Spanish-American War and took control of Spanish territories, including Cuba. The island became little more than a US protectorate. Cuban leaders consulted Washington when they wanted to make decisions, and Cuban laws were designed to protect US business interests.

An Armed Revolt

In April 1952, former president Fulgencio Batista overthrew the Cuban government and set up a corrupt dictatorship. Most Cubans lived in extreme poverty. Almost at once, Batista faced armed revolt. In 1953 the guerrilla leader Fidel Castro attacked the army's Moncada Barracks in a failed attempt to overthrow the dictator.

FIDEL CASTRO

Fidel Castro Ruz was the son of a wealthy plantation owner and his maid. He first became involved in antigovernment protests as a law student at the University of Havana. After forcing Batista from power in January 1959, Castro became prime minister. He set out to restore Cuba's national identity. He nationalized many industries, which brought him into conflict with the United States. He became president in 1976 but retired in 2008 because of ill health.

Surrounded by his followers, Fidel Castro (center) makes a speech after seizing power in Cuba.

Huge flames erupt from a gas pipe in Havana in 1959 after rebels caused an explosion during the run-up to the revolution.

Granmá

Castro was jailed for two years, but became a hero for many Cubans. On his release in 1955, he and his brother, Raúl, went to Mexico and the United States to raise support for a guerrilla war against Batista. The Argentine revolutionary Ernesto "Che" Guevara joined them. In December 1956, the Castros, Guevara, and more than 80 rebels sailed from Mexico to Cuba in a leaky, overloaded yacht named *Granmá* that barely survived the journey.

The Castros and Che Guevara made their way to the Sierra Maestra. From there they spent two years launching guerrilla attacks on Batista's forces.

The casino of Havana's Riviera Hotel is quiet after the revolution ended the US tourism that had given Cuba such financial success.

CUBA AND THE USA

After the United States had liberated Cuba from Spanish rule, it virtually ruled the island for the next 60 years. As drinking and gambling were more strictly controlled at home in the 1920s and 1930s, US tourists flocked to Cuba, where they could drink and gamble freely. US businesses were happy to work in Cuba thanks to favorable tax breaks. But many poor Cubans resented being a vacation outpost of the United States. They also objected to Washington's influence in Cuban affairs.

High Profile Campaign

Castro broadcast radio messages to his fellow Cubans and gave interviews to foreign journalists. Soon he attracted hundreds of people to join his rebel band, who were known as *los barbudos* ("the bearded ones"). Batista's men put up little resistance. When the United States imposed an economic embargo on Cuba, Batista's position was weakened still further. On January 1, 1959, the dictator fled the island. A week later, Castro rode triumphantly into the capital, Havana.

Cubans in the United States

While many Cubans rejoiced as Fidel Castro rode into Havana, others were outraged. Castro's policies threatened their US-influenced way of life. They fled to Miami, Florida. They hoped exile would be temporary, but many of their families would still be in Florida over 50 years later.

Cuban refugees visit the relocation department of a Catholic charity. Relatively few of the exiles wanted to move anywhere but Miami.

A store in Miami displays a photograph of President Kennedy, who many Cuban exiles saw as a leader who would stand up to Castro.

The first wave of emigrants left Cuba in 1959, after Castro came to power. Many Cubans did not believe Castro's assurances that he was not a communist. A second wave of emigration began in 1961, when Castro began a program of nationalization and seized all private land. Worried parents sent more than 14,000 children to the United States to avoid possible communist indoctrination, or influence.

Little Havana

Most Cubans settled in Miami, Florida, in an area that became known as "Little Havana." Others moved to California, New Jersey, and New York.

POLITICS IN EXILE

The high concentrations of Cuban exiles in Miami, Florida, and Union City, New Jersey, formed political groups to make their voice heard. The majority of Cuban–Americans supported the US embargo against Cuba and were fervently anti-Castro. They wanted the US government to get rid of him by any means. Other groups were less opposed to Castro but still supported the embargo. There was never an opposition in exile united against Castro's regime.

Bay of Pigs Invasion

The uneasy relationship between Castro's Cuba and the United States had lasted for two years when John F. Kennedy was inaugurated as the 35th president on January 19, 1961. One of the first problems the new president had to deal with was a secret US plan to overthrow Fidel Castro and his government.

A Cuban soldier guards one of six B-26 bombers shot down in the invasion. The planes were proof of US involvement in the operation.

Castro had been a constant irritant to the United States. He had nationalized the oil and sugar industries, and had seized the assets of the US firms who controlled them. The then president, Dwight D. Eisenhower, ordered a sugar embargo. The United States, which was the largest importer of Cuban sugar, would no longer buy it. Eisenhower also ordered the Central Intelligence Agency (CIA) to come up with a secret plan to topple Castro.

CIA Tactics

The CIA was optimistic. In 1954 it had helped overthrow President Arbenz of Guatemala.

Cuban soldiers gather in Havana to face a rumored invasion in January 1961— just 12 weeks before the Bay of Pigs invasion came.

JFK'S ROLE

The new president had only been in office for three months when the Bay of Pigs disaster happened. Although he had only inherited the plan, Kennedy had made basic errors. But the humiliation taught him a painful lesson. He learned not to trust the so-called experts completely and to question them more. He had accepted the CIA's false assumption about the Cuban people's loyalty without question, for example. Such lessons would serve him well during the missile crisis.

The CIA first planned to assassinate Castro. One idea was to use exploding cigars—Castro was a famous cigar smoker—or poisoned milkshakes. Instead they decided to organize a ground invasion by Cuban exiles. The CIA believed that the invasion force would be joined by thousands of disillusioned Cubans who would rise up against Castro's oppression. It trained volunteer exiles in the jungles of Guatemala.

A Fiasco!

President Kennedy reluctantly agreed that the plan should go ahead. On April 17, 1961, some 1,400 members of the anti-Castro Cuban Brigade landed at the Bay of Pigs on Cuba's south coast.

Under its director Allen Dulles, the CIA came up with ambitious—and sometimes crazy—plans to topple Fidel Castro.

EYES ONLY

4 October 1962

MEMORANDUM FOR RECORD

SUBJECT: Minutes of Meeting of the Special Group (Augmented) on Operation MONGOOSE, 4 October 1962

PRESENT: The Attorney General; Mr. Johnson; Mr. Gilpatric, General Taylor, General Lansdale; Mr. McCone and General Carter; Mr. Wilson

1. The Attorney General opened the meeting by saying that higher authority is concerned about progress on the MONGOOSE program and feels that more priority should be given to trying to mount sabotage operations. The Attorney General said that he wondered if a new look is not required at this time in view of the meager results, especially in the sabotage field. He urged that "massive activity" be mounted within the entire MONGOOSE framework. There was a good deal of discussion about this, and General Lansdale said that another attempt will be made against the major target which has been the object of three unsuccessful missions, and that approximately six new ones are in the planning stage.

Mr. Johnson said that "massive activity" would have to appear to come from within. He also said that he hopes soon to be able to present to the Group a plan for giving Cuban exiles more of a free hand, with the full realization that this would give more visibility to their activities. On this latter point, Mr. McCone said that he reserves judgment as to the feasibility and desirability of such a program. (Mr. Johnson agreed that he has reservations as well.)

2. Mr. McCone then said that he gets the impression that high levels of the government want to get on with activity but still wish to retain a low noise level. He does not believe that this will be possible. Any sabotage would be blamed on the United States. In this connection, he cited the enormous number of telephone calls that had been directed at CIA at the time that the skin divers landed in Eastern Cuba and at the time Cuban exile students shot up the apartment house. He urged that responsible officials be prepared to accept a higher noise level if they want to get on with operations.

In partial rebuttal, the Attorney General said that the reasons people were so concerned at the times mentioned were: (a) the fact that the skin divers were Americans, and (b) that the student

DECLASSIFIED

TOP SECRET

EYES ONLY

These notes record a secret meeting held in October 1961 to discuss US policy toward Cuba.

A Cuban army of 35,000 soldiers, equipped with Soviet-built artillery and tanks, was waiting for them. With no aerial support from the United States, the invasion force was left to fend for itself. The expected uprising by local Cubans did not happen. After three days' fighting, the Cuban Brigade surrendered.

A Humiliation

The failure of the invasion made it impossible to hide the involvement of the CIA. The humiliating defeat made the United States look deceitful and incompetent. For Castro, the invasion strengthened his relationship with the Soviet Union—and paved the way for the missile crisis.

OPERATION MONGOOSE

The secret CIA operation against Castro was code-named Operation Mongoose. It plotted various ways to kill Castro. In one crazy scheme, special salt would be put in Castro's shoes that would make his hair and beard fall out. In theory, this would make him look so unattractive the Cuban people would reject him as their leader. Overall, the CIA was so determined to get rid of Castro that it failed to appreciate the huge loyalty most Cubans felt toward him.

The Soviet Union and Cuba

Nikita Khrushchev embraces Fidel Castro as the two men meet at the United Nations in 1960.

In the late 1950s, many Americans initially approved of Fidel Castro. They saw him as a romantic hero trying to overthrow an unpopular dictator. They did not see him as a communist. By the early 1960s, the US view of Castro had changed. He had become the communist in their backyard and appeared to be an ally of their greatest enemy, the Soviet Union.

Khrushchev (waving) saw that it would be strategically valuable to have an ally as close to the United States as Cuba.

In some ways, the United States helped create the close relationship between Cuba and the Soviet Union. Castro had come to power as a nationalist rather than a communist. But when he nationalized the oil industry, President Eisenhower responded by cutting Cuban sugar imports by 95 percent.

Growing Links

The Soviet Union immediately agreed to buy the sugar. Cuba's economic links with the Soviets led to greater political links. On December 19, 1960, Castro proclaimed Cuba's solidarity with the Soviet Union. In retaliation, Eisenhower cut diplomatic ties with Cuba. The stage was set for a showdown.

NIKITA KHRUSHCHEV

The Soviet leader came to power after the death of the dictator Joseph Stalin. Khrushchev presented his US counterparts with a challenge. He was by turns friendly and aggressive. He had visited the United States in September 1959. To the irritation of the Americans, the Soviets had landed a rocket on the moon the previous day. Khrushchev boasted about this feat, while criticizing capitalism for being wasteful. He constantly argued that communism was a far superior political system.

Missiles in Cuba

The United States viewed the contacts between Cuba and the Soviet Union with alarm. It would be a huge threat if the Soviets used Cuba as a military base. In August 1962, a US spy plane took the first photographs of Soviet surface-to-air missiles in Cuba.

In October 1962, CIA pictures taken from a spy plane revealed that the Soviet Union had installed nuclear missiles in Cuba.

CHERRY PICKER

LAUNCH PAD WITH ERECTOR

LAUNCH PAD WITH ERECTOR

MISSILE READY BLDGS

OXIDIZER VEHICLES

FUELING VEHICLES

FRUIT SET WITH VERTICAL NETTING

7 MISSILE TRANSPORTERS

PROBABLE LIGHT AA POSITIONS

SUPPORT AREA U C

POSSIBLE ACQUISITION RADAR & ASSOCIATED EQUIPMENT

MISSILES ON LAUNCHERS

Aerial reconnaissance suggested to US analysts that the Soviet missiles were only weeks away from being ready to fire.

The US government's worst fear about the growing links between Cuba and the Soviet Union was that Cuba would somehow be included in the Soviet military system. The island was so close to the United States that missiles fired from there could strike US targets before they could be intercepted.

US intelligence noticed an increase in shipping in Cuban waters. They guessed that the Soviet Union was supplying arms to Castro—but they believed the missiles were for defense, after the Bay of Pigs attack. They also assumed any weapons were conventional.

US MISSILES IN TURKEY

In May 1962, the United States had finished deploying Jupiter nuclear missiles to Turkey. They were there to make sure the nuclear defenses of the North Atlantic Treaty Organization (NATO) balanced those of the Soviet Union and its allies. The Jupiters were outdated weapons, but their presence annoyed Khrushchev. He might have sent nuclear weapons to Cuba as a bargaining tool in order to get the Jupiters removed from Turkey.

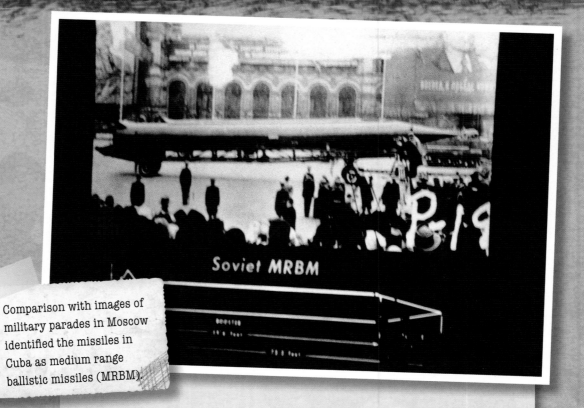

Soviet MRBM

Comparison with images of military parades in Moscow identified the missiles in Cuba as medium range ballistic missiles (MRBM).

Khrushchev would surely realize that basing nuclear weapons in Cuba would be a provocative move. The US government believed there was no reason why he would take such a risk.

Operation Anadyr

The Soviet Union saw things differently. Khrushchev feared that the United States would attempt another invasion of Cuba. The Americans might use nuclear weapons, so the Soviets believed they needed nuclear weapons themselves. They even planned to send a full battle-ready force to Cuba in what they called Operation Anadyr. In the end, the Soviets scaled down their deployment to avoid provoking the Americans—but they still sent the nuclear weapons.

Startling Discovery

On August 29, 1962, a high-altitude U-2 spy plane photographed SAM (surface-to-air missile) sites in Cuba, with missile boats and other weapons. On October 14, another spy plane photographed a new threat: a nuclear missile site in western Cuba.

Emergency Briefing

On October 16, President Kennedy took part in a security briefing while he was still in his pajamas. The United States' worst nightmare had come to pass. The Soviets had shipped nuclear missiles to Cuba and were readying them for deployment. The Cuban missile crisis had begun.

KHRUSHCHEV'S MOTIVES

Historians still speculate on why Khrushchev sent nuclear weapons to Cuba. In his memoirs, he said his primary motive was defending Cuba against a possible US invasion, which seemed more likely after the Bay of Pigs fiasco. Khrushchev was irritated that Western powers had not withdrawn completely from Berlin in Germany. It was under Khrushchev that the Berlin Wall had been erected in August 1961, dividing the city.

SOVIET SHIP POLTAVA ENROUTE TO CUBA
15 SEPTEMBER 1962

ПОЛТАВА

This CIA photograph shows a Soviet vessel carrying missiles and other military supplies to Cuba in September 1962.

Reaction in the United States

After Kennedy was briefed on October 16, 1962, he immediately called an emergency committee of his closest advisors. They would meet in secret over the next days to debate their response to the Soviet move. Get it wrong, and they knew that the world's first nuclear war might be imminent.

Visitors to the White House check their belongings as part of increased security measures during the missile crisis.

Robert McNamara, seen here during the Vietnam War in 1965, was secretary of defense during the missile crisis.

Three hours after National Security Advisor McGeorge Bundy briefed Kennedy, the president assembled a group of senior officials. They would become known as the Executive Committee of the National Security Council (ExComm). Robert McNamara, the secretary of defense, reported that the Soviet missiles could be operational within two weeks.

Two Options

ExComm decided that the Soviet missiles had to be removed without delay. The question was how. Their discussions quickly came down to two likely options. The first

HAWKS VS DOVES

ExComm was made up of Kennedy's closest advisors. They included his brother, Attorney General Robert Kennedy, Secretary of State Dean Rusk, and Robert McNamara. The joint Chiefs of Staff and the head of the CIA were also members. Initially, the president sided with the "hawks," who favored air strikes. His brother was a "dove"; he was eager to avoid any military aggression. Eventually, Robert Kennedy's blockade option won favor, and the balance on ExComm moved toward the doves.

Soviet ambassador Anatoly Dobrynin (left) and foreign minister Andrei Gromyko (center) meet President Kennedy on October 18, 1961.

was air strikes to destroy the missile sites. The second was a naval blockade to prevent more military supplies or men from arriving. Initially, Kennedy favored the first option. But heavy air attacks would involve high casualties. They would also be a clear signal that the United States was at war. Kennedy therefore turned to the second option: a blockade.

Soviet Surprise

On October 18, Kennedy held a long-arranged meeting with Soviet foreign minister Andrei Gromyko. He did not tell Gromyko that he knew about the missile bases. Gromyko reported back to Moscow that no US invasion of Cuba seemed likely in the near future.

Imposing a Blockade

Meanwhile the Americans prepared the blockade. They were so worried about provoking the Soviets that they called it a "quarantine," which sounded less aggressive. On October 22, Kennedy made a TV broadcast to tell Americans—and the world—what the United States knew about the Soviet bases. He said that the quarantine would begin at 10:00 A.M. on October 24. US forces around the world were already on standby.

KENNEDY'S SPEECH

In his broadcast, Kennedy explained that the administration was determined to make sure the missiles were removed from Cuba. He announced a quarantine on all military weapons being shipped to Cuba. Any missile launch from Cuba against the West, he added, would be seen as an attack by the Soviet Union.

President Kennedy is shown making his TV address on October 22, when he told Americans there were Soviet missiles in Cuba.

The US Quarantine

President John F. Kennedy signs the order imposing the "quarantine" on Cuba on October 23, 1961.

When President Kennedy addressed the nation on October 22, 1962, three Soviet ships carrying military hardware were close to Cuba. Another nine vessels were crossing the Atlantic. The US naval "quarantine" was intended to stop them.

Kennedy was still considering using air strikes. But the commander of US Air Force Tactical Air Command, General Walter Sweeney, could not guarantee that bombing would destroy all the missiles on Cuba. Neither air strikes nor a blockade could rid Cuba of all the weapons already in place there.

The Wrong Choice?

Just before Kennedy went on TV, he briefed congressional leaders on the situation. Many thought the "quarantine" was too weak a response to the crisis. But Kennedy argued that he could not risk provoking the Soviet leader

TASS STATEMENT

On the morning of October 23, 1962, the Soviet news agency TASS issued a statement. It accused Kennedy of breaking international law with the blockade, and of piracy. It stated that the weapons sited on Cuba were purely defensive and not to attack the United States. The statement ended with a grim warning that US actions might lead "to catastrophic consequences for world peace."

President Kennedy and Secretary of Defense Robert McNamara discuss the crisis outside the Oval Office in the White House.

A photograph taken from inside the White House shows antiwar protestors in the street outside at the height of the crisis.

into a response: "If we go into Cuba, we have to realize that we have taken the chance that these missiles, which are ready to fire, won't be fired." It was, he admitted, "a gamble."

Under Quarantine

The blockade came into effect at 10:00 A.M. (Eastern time) on Wednesday, October 24, 1962. The blockade was formed in the shape of an arc 500 miles (800 km) from Cape Maysi, on Cuba's eastern coast. The location was deliberately chosen to be out of range of Soviet IL-28 bombers on Cuba. The blockade comprised 12 destroyers from the Second Fleet's Task Force 136, supplemented by the aircraft carrier USS *Essex*, with further anti-submarine squadrons on alert on the islands of Bermuda and Puerto Rico.

A Wise Decision

Kennedy judged carefully how to implement the blockade. He ordered the US Navy to allow the first ship to reach the blockade—an oil tanker—to pass. An East German passenger ship was also allowed to pass. Meanwhile the Americans bolstered the blockade to include 27 ships forming two lines, "Walnut" and "Chestnut."

The Soviets Blink

Then ExComm received news that the Soviet ships closest to the blockade were turning back. Dean Rusk said to McGeorge Bundy, "We're eyeball to eyeball and I think the other fellow just blinked."

ExComm meets to discuss the crisis on October 29, 1962, by which time it had become clear the Soviets were backing down.

EXCOMM

ExComm stands for Executive Committee of the National Security Council. It was assembled in total secrecy by McGeorge Bundy, the national security advisor, to advise President Kennedy during the crisis. Over a period of 16 days, the group met at least once a day. Early on in the crisis, Kennedy looked to the group for ideas; later on, he tended to use them as a sounding board for his own ideas.

The Nuclear Arsenal

Since the first nuclear device was tested in Alamagordo, New Mexico, on July 16, 1945, the world had lived with the fear of the destructive capabilities of atomic weapons. The Cuban missile crisis was such a tense period because people believed that both sides had enough nuclear weapons to destroy the other completely.

Both superpowers had created arsenals of missiles like this US Titan that could carry nuclear warheads between continents.

Nuclear warfare was a terrifying prospect. Robert McNamara estimated that a small nuclear war would kill 25 million Americans.

The Soviet Union tested a nuclear bomb in 1949. The two superpowers raced to build more powerful weapons. By the 1960s, hydrogen bombs (H-bombs) could wipe out whole cities. There were three types of nuclear weapons: land-based intercontinental ballistic missiles (ICBMs), submarine-launched ballistic missiles (SLBMs), and short-range missiles launched by bombers.

MAD

Such weapons were so powerful that it was almost unthinkable that they would actually be fired. A military principle known as Mutually Assured Destruction (MAD) argued that if one side attacked, the other would retaliate. Both countries would be destroyed.

ICBMS

The Soviet Union concentrated its nuclear power in ICBMs. They were the most accurate of the new weapons and carried the largest warheads. In the 1960s, the technology did not yet exist to intercept missiles. Once a missile was launched from Cuba, it would hit its target within 30 minutes. The Soviet SS-9 Scarp had a range of 5,500 nautical miles. The Americans believed it was designed to knock out their Minutemen ICBM launch control centers (LCCs).

The World Holds Its Breath

With the blockade in place, the United States and the rest of the world waited to see what would happen next. Nobody knew how the Soviets would react when one of their ships was stopped. At 10:30 A.M. the US Navy stopped a Soviet tanker. It was searched before it was allowed to continue, as Kennedy had instructed.

The US destroyer *John R. Pierce* was part of the blockade force. It turned back a Lebanese ship on October 26, 1962.

Demonstrators in Washington, DC, urge Kennedy not to be too aggressive in his handling of the crisis.

Late on October 26, the US State Department received a letter from Khrushchev. In return for the United States promising not to invade Cuba, Khrushchev would remove the Soviet missiles. ExComm was debating the message when a more aggressive letter arrived. Now Khrushchev demanded that the US withdraw its missiles from Turkey in exchange for the Soviet withdrawal of missiles from Cuba.

ExComm Panics

Members of ExComm panicked. The hawks, including Dean Rusk, did not want to give in over Turkey. The doves (Robert Kennedy

THE LAST SATURDAY?

By the evening of Saturday, October 27, 1962, ExComm had played all its cards. Would Khrushchev accept the US deal? If he delayed, the members of ExComm believed the United States would have no choice but to attack Cuba, as the Soviet missiles could be launched at any moment. The crisis was at its height. Secretary of Defense Robert McNamara later recalled how much he savored the clear fall air that evening "because I thought it was the last Saturday I would ever see."

and Robert McNamara) thought that risking a global nuclear war over the missiles in Turkey was crazy. The debate continued into Saturday.

A Missing Plane

Now the situation became even more serious. A US U-2 spy plane failed to return from a flight over Cuba. Should the Americans retaliate? Kennedy hesitated, knowing the potential gravity of the situation. Khrushchev's reaction was also cautious. He had given orders that no US aircraft should be fired upon, so he did not understand how a U-2 had been shot down.

Demonstrators in Moscow protest what they see as US imperialism in the imposition of the blockade on Cuba.

Peace protestors sit down to block a street in London as they urge the US government not to go to war over Cuba.

INTERNATIONAL REACTION

The United Nations (UN) had an active role in the missile crisis. On October 17, 1962, acting Secretary-General U Thant sent both Kennedy and Khrushchev a proposal to end the standoff. He wrote that "the rest of the world is an interested party," and asked that neither man do anything to make the situation worse. He asked representatives of both sides to meet at the UN in New York. Their talks went on in parallel to the decisive talks in Washington.

A Clever Solution

Eventually Kennedy decided to ignore both the shooting down of the U-2 and the second of Khrushchev's letters. Instead he responded to the first letter and accepted its more conciliatory terms. He sent his brother, Attorney General Robert Kennedy, to meet the Soviet ambassador, Anatoly Dobrynin. Kennedy told Dobrynin unofficially that the US would remove the missiles from Turkey—but that this was not to be part of the formal agreement to end the crisis.

Khrushchev Backs Down

A Soviet vessel steams away from the exclusion zone with its cargo on deck left plainly visible for US aerial reconnaissance.

Before he had written his first letter to Kennedy, Khrushchev began to have doubts about taking on the United States. He wanted to find a way out of the crisis that would preserve Soviet dignity, but backing down was a PR disaster and ultimately cost him his job.

A US Polaris submarine sets off to sea. Such submarines provided mobile launch platforms for US nuclear missiles.

By Saturday, October 27, Khrushchev was more confident. Five days of the US blockade had passed without a clash. He hoped the enemy might make more concessions, so he wrote his more aggressive second letter. But the shooting down of the U-2 again made him nervous.

End of the Crisis

On Sunday, October 28, 1962, Moscow announced that its missiles in Cuba would be dismantled and shipped back to the Soviet Union. Kennedy ended the blockade. As promised, the US missiles in Turkey were secretly withdrawn six months later.

NUCLEAR ESCALATION

After the crisis was over, the Americans discovered that some of the Soviet missiles in Cuba were fully operational. They could have been launched at any moment. This had been the government's main worry. Any false step could have led to nuclear war. Coming so close to a disaster led the superpowers to set up a "hot line" teleprinter link between the White House and the Kremlin. They hoped that would help prevent any future misunderstandings.

After the Crisis

Life changed dramatically after the Cuban Missile Crisis. Political tensions continued between Cuba and the United States, but US relations with the Soviet Union improved dramatically. But the air of optimism was shattered by the assassination of President Kennedy.

Anti-Castro Cuban exiles train in the Florida Everglades in 1963; they still hoped to launch a military invasion of Cuba.

Watched by President Lyndon Johnson (right), Secretary of State Dean Rusk signs the latest in a line of nuclear treaties in 1968.

Fidel Castro refused to let arms inspectors into Cuba. As a result, as Soviet ships left Cuban waters soldiers pulled back tarpaulins so that US aircraft could see the missiles on deck.

A Way Forward

Having come so close to nuclear war, both sides agreed to set up a "hot line." They also agreed to ban some nuclear weapons testing. The Limited Test Ban Treaty (LTBT) was signed by the United States, the Soviet Union, and the United Kingdom in August 1963. The treaty marked the first pause in the arms race. It led to a series of further bans on nuclear development.

DEATH OF JFK

On November 22, 1963, President John F. Kennedy was shot and killed in Dallas, Texas. His approval rating had soared after the missile crisis to over 70 percent. Now Americans were stunned that the man who saved them from disaster was dead. There were suggestions that anti-Castro Cubans were involved in the killing, because they believed Kennedy was not firm enough about Cuba. The allegation was never proven.

TIMELINE

1959   January 1: Fidel Castro comes to power in Cuba after leading a revolution against Fulgencio Batista.

1960   December 19: Fidel Castro proclaims Cuba's solidarity with the Soviet Union.

1961   January 3: After Castro nationalizes US industries in Cuba, the United States breaks all diplomatic relations with Cuba.

January 19: John F. Kennedy is inaugurated as the 35th president of the United States.

April 17: Some 1,400 members of the Cuban Brigade land at the Bay of Pigs in Cuba in an invasion supported by the CIA; it is a military disaster—some 100 invaders are killed; the others surrender after three days.

June 3: President Kennedy meets Soviet leader Nikita Khrushchev for the only time, at a summit meeting in Vienna, Austria.

1962   July 27: Castro claims that the Soviets are helping Cuba defend itself against further US invasions.

September 11: Soviet foreign minister Andrei Gromyko warns the United Nations that a US attack on Cuba would lead to war with the Soviet Union.

October 14: A U-2 spy plane flying over western Cuba photographs sites housing missiles, which next day are identified as Soviet medium-range ballistic missiles.

1962   **October 16: National Security Advisor McGeorge Bundy briefs Kennedy about the missiles; Kennedy summons the first meeting of ExComm to discuss the US response to the Cuban Missile Crisis.**

October 17: Another U-2 flight over Cuba discovers intercontinental ballistic nuclear missiles.

October 18: Kennedy meets Soviet foreign minister Andrei Gromyko, but does not reveal that the Americans know about the missiles in Cuba.

October 21: Kennedy decides to impose a quarantine of Cuba after US Air Force leaders refuse to guarantee all the missiles can be destroyed with air strikes.

October 22: Kennedy briefs congressional leaders before going on TV to tell Americans about the presence of Soviet missiles in Cuba.

October 23: Kennedy receives a letter from Khrushchev and decides to delay the full implementation of the blockade.

October 24: Soviet ships heading to Cuba slow down or turn around.

October 25: ExComm discusses offering to withdraw US missiles from Turkey if the Soviets withdraw their missiles from Cuba.

October 26: Khrushchev writes to Kennedy, offering to withdraw the missiles in return for a US promise never to invade Cuba.

October 27: In another letter, Khrushchev now proposes that US missiles are withdrawn from Turkey; a US U-2 spy plane is shot down over Cuba; Kennedy writes to Khrushchev, agreeing to a commitment not to invade Cuba.

October 28: Khrushchev announces on the radio in Moscow that the missiles will be withdrawn from Cuba.

GLOSSARY

ballistic Describes a missile that is powered by a motor as it ascends, but that free-falls to its target through the force of gravity.

bloc A group of nations that acts together.

blockade The use of ships and other methods to prevent vessels or aircraft entering or leaving a country.

communists People who support a society where all property is owned by the state, which in turn supports the welfare of all its citizens.

conciliatory Describes a gesture of friendship made to try to overcome someone's distrust.

conventional Describes traditional gunpowder weapons.

embargo A government's prohibition of trade with a foreign country.

exile Someone who lives outside their native country.

guerrilla Someone who fights by irregular means such as ambush, sabotage, and assassination.

nationalist Someone who believes that a people should be able to govern themselves.

nationalize To take businesses from private into government ownership.

nuclear A weapon that generates huge amounts of energy by splitting or fusing the nucleii of atoms.

retaliation Reacting against an attack in a similar manner.

strategic Something that is related to an overall conflict, rather than to a short-term victory in a battle.

totalitarian Describes a form of government in which the political authorities have complete control.

warhead The armed part at the tip of a missile that carries high explosives or a nuclear system.

FURTHER INFORMATION

Books

Byrne, Paul J. *The Cuban Missile Crisis: To the Brink of War* (Snapshots in History). Compass Point Books, 2006.

Hennessey, Kate. *Castro's Cuba* (History Firsthand). Greenhaven Press, 2004.

Jeffrey, Gary. *The Cuban Missile Crisis* (Graphic Modern History: Cold War Conflicts). Crabtree Publishing Company, 2013.

Senker, Cath. *Kennedy and the Cuban Missile Crisis* (Days of Decision). Raintree, 2013.

Stein, R. Conrad. *Cuban Missile Crisis: In the Shadow of Nuclear War* (America's Living History). Enslow Publishers, 2008.

Wagner, Heather Lehr. *The Cuban Missile Crisis* (Milestones in American History). Chelsea House Publishers, 2011.

Websites

www.jfklibrary.org/JFK/JFK-in-History/Cuban-Missile-Crisis.aspx
JFK Library exhibit about the president and the crisis.

www.history.com/topics/cuban-missile-crisis
History.com page of links about the crisis.

www.spartacus.schoolnet.co.uk/COLDcubanmissile.htm
Spartacus Educational page with links to biographies and other articles.

www.bbc.co.uk/news/magazine-20068265
BBC News article with an overview of the crisis and its significance.

Publisher's note to educators and parents: Our editors have carefully reviewed these websites to ensure that they are suitable for students. Many websites change frequently, however, and we cannot guarantee that a site's future contents will continue to meet our high standards of quality and educational value. Be advised that students should be closely supervised whenever they access the Internet.

INDEX